Congratulations

(09).

MB015 SPD067 BA030
B STA003 CGN PD=STAMFORD CONN 6 705A EDE=
=RONNIE RABINOVTIZ=
    817 NEW YORK AVE SHEBOYGAN WIS=

CONGRATULATIONS SORRY TO HAVE DELAYED MESSAGE
HAVE BEEN OUT OF CITY AM ALWAYS PROUD OF YOUR ACHIEVEMENTS
CONTINUED GOOD LUCK=
    JACKIE ROBINSON=

BY WESTERN UNION

ALWAYS, JACKIE

THE TRUE STORY OF A BOY AND HIS BASEBALL HERO

Ron Rabinovitz & J. Patrick Lewis

illustrated by John Thompson

Creative Editions

Text copyright © 2020 by J. Patrick Lewis · Illustrations copyright © 2020 by John Thompson · Photographs by Getty Images (The Frent Collection/Corbis Historical) · Edited by Amy Novesky and Kate Riggs; designed by Rita Marshall · Published in 2020 by Creative Editions · P.O. Box 227, Mankato, MN 56002 USA · Creative Editions is an imprint of The Creative Company · www.thecreativecompany.us
Library of Congress Cataloging-in-Publication Data · Names: Lewis, J. Patrick, author. / Rabinovitz, Ron, contributor. / Thompson, John, illustrator. · Title: Always, Jackie / by J. Patrick Lewis, with Ron Rabinovitz; illustrated by John Thompson. Includes bibliographical references. Summary: The unbelievable yet true story of how an eight-year-old white kid from Sheboygan, Wisconsin, met the legendary Jackie Robinson in the 1950s—and how the two became lifelong friends. · Identifiers: LCCN 2019027701 / ISBN 978-1-56846-307-0 · Subjects: LCSH: Robinson, Jackie, 1919–72—Juvenile literature. / Baseball players—United States—Biography—Juvenile literature. / African American baseball players—Biography—Juvenile literature. / Friendship—Juvenile literature. / Rabinovitz, Ronnie—Juvenile literature. · Classification: LCC GV865.R6 R33 2020 / DDC 796.357092 [B]—dc23 / First edition

9 8 7 6 5 4 3 2 1

FOREWORD

Long ago, when baseball was still our national pastime, a man grew into a giant. Who was he? The first black ballplayer in the major leagues. Exceptionally gifted, Jackie Robinson quickly became a household name. And long after a distinguished career on and off the diamond, decades after his death, his legend continues to grow. Along the bruising road to glory, he found a friend in the heart of the country—a youngster with curveball hopes and fastball dreams named Ronnie Rabinovitz.

IMAGINE A SEVEN-YEAR-OLD from Anywhere, U.S.A.—or Sheboygan, Wisconsin, to be exact. Brooklyn Dodgers cap on head, baseball mitt in hand, the boy would race outside after school to play pitcher, batter, and announcer all in one. Though his younger sister Judi sometimes roamed the outfield behind him, Ronnie Rabinovitz kept his eyes focused on the most formidable of World Series foes: the garage door.

His bedroom was like an artful Dodger's dugout, his backyard as green and smooth as a miniature Ebbets Field. In those days, nearly every American schoolboy followed a favorite team, but for Ronnie, it wasn't simply a pastime but an obsession.

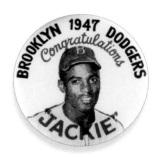

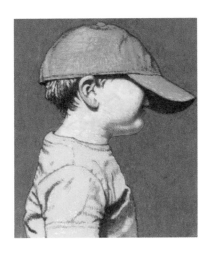

WHEN RONNIE WAS STILL A TODDLER, a revolu-
tion rocked baseball. The first black man in history
put on a major-league uniform, changing the face
of sports and this country. Jackie Robinson, a four-
sport star athlete, endured a lifetime of prejudice,
yet he continued to play the game he loved most
amidst arrows of insults in stadiums of bigotry.

BLACK CATS tossed from the stands were the least of it. Threatening letters arrived almost daily. Some pitchers were told to throw at his head. Restaurants that welcomed his fellow teammates refused to serve a black man.

THE BOY had his own experience with prejudice. As a midwestern Jewish kid, Ronnie, as well as his family, faced cruel anti-Semitic comments. Even classmates he thought were his friends turned their backs on him.

Yet the man and the boy persevered—Jackie on the diamond and Ronnie in his love of the game, the Brooklyn Dodgers, and every pitch to his hero, the unrivaled second baseman. Though separated by age,

race, religion, and geography, this unimaginable pair became lifelong friends all on account of a game— baseball—and a man, the boy's beloved father. Ronnie and Jackie were soon to meet at the crossroads of hope and history.

David Rabinovitz inspired his son's deep admiration for Jackie. One day he wrote to the baseball sensation to say how much the boy would love to meet his idol. David never expected a reply. After all, Jackie inhabited the planet of the few and the famous.

WHEN RONNIE DISCOVERED what his dad had done, he became the postman's best pal: hugging the mailbox daily, waiting endlessly for a letter, a postcard, anything at all. And when it finally arrived—did it come by moonbeam?—he brushed off the glitter and nearly melted: Jackie—the one and only Jackie Robinson!—said he hoped to meet Ronnie and his father the next time the Dodgers were in town.

Then came the magical moment: Milwaukee County Stadium, 1953. Brooklyn's invincible Boys of Summer, the men of Flatbush, were playing catch right there in front of father and son. Duke Snider, Pee Wee Reese, Roy Campanella, Don Newcombe, and Gil Hodges. Number 42, the brightest star of all, hit for a double and a single, stole a base, and grew a foot and a half in Ronnie's eyes that day.

AFTER THE GAME, David and Ronnie, hearts racing, made their way to the locker room entrance, where a sign read: "WARNING: DO NOT ENTER. You could go to jail." Reporters walked in and out, but not the Rabinovitzes. Not without a pass. All they could do was wait—agonizing torture for any eight-year-old. The door finally opened! The players were filing out, but where was Jackie? How could Ronnie have missed that patented Robinson smile? Then . . . then . . .

There it was!

"Hi, Jackie!" he shouted. "I'm Ronnie Rabinovitz. Do you remember me?"

"Of course I do!" Jackie said. "I remember the letter your dad wrote to me on 'lawyer's stationery.'"

Ronnie's heart thudded like a catcher's mitt. When he stammered that he would write to him soon, Jackie said, "GOOD!" The boy felt like "a rocket soaring above the earth." And so began the unlikely friendship between a baseball icon and a Jewish kid from Sheboygan, Wisconsin, who was about to experience a childhood like no other.

WHAT YOUNG MAN can say the other guest of honor at his 10th birthday party was the great Jackie Robinson? Or that he was taken by the hand inside a major-league dressing room by the man himself to get a baseball signed by every Brooklyn Dodger? Or that he was given the key to a city—Manitowoc, Wisconsin—originally presented to Jackie, who asked Ronnie to keep it safe for him?

In October of 1956, Jackie played his last major-league game. It had been an amazing career, spanning 10 emotional seasons. Over that time, Jackie stole 197 bases (including 19 steals of home), hit 137 home runs, drove in 734 runs, and wrote more than 20 letters to young Ronnie. The most unlikely of friends had become forever pen pals.

Through Ronnie's high school and college years and beyond, he and Jackie continued to call or write each other, hoping to never lose touch. And all the while, Ronnie remained Sheboygan's #1 baseball statistician, recording every Dodger hiccup and sneeze, even after Jackie retired, and even after the team had so disappointed him by moving to Los Angeles.

IN 1972, the two friends met for lunch in Manhattan. Though only 53, the Dodger star, nearly blind now, had suffered from diabetes for almost two decades. Grief over Jackie Jr., his 24-year-old son who had died in a car accident, seemed to worsen his heart condition. As Ronnie helped Jackie down the restaurant stairs, he was heartbroken to see his idol so seriously ill, for this was the man who had once danced down base paths like Fred Astaire, leaping along the edge to legend.

Six months later, on October 24, 1972, Jackie Robinson died. Ronnie was devastated. He expressed the depth of his sorrow to Rachel, Jackie's widow, who knew just how much their 19-year friendship had meant to her husband.

"They say Babe Ruth changed baseball, but Jackie Robinson changed America," Ronnie has said. "As I grew older, I realized how much more he was than baseball. There was no Martin Luther King Jr. at his side, no Rosa Parks at his side, no Civil Rights Movement. He fought the good fight alone."

AS BREEZES WHISTLE through the stadium, men on the mound, in the dugout, and on the field have something in common. A little girl points and asks her father, "Why does everyone have '42' on the backs of their uniforms?"

"'Happens every April 15th, sweetheart. They're honoring the memory of Jackie Robinson, who played his first game in the majors on this date in 1947. Some say he's still out there somewhere, turning a double play or stealing second once more."

Or hitting another home run in a young child's heart.

EPILOGUE

For many years now, Ron Rabinovitz—husband, father, grandfather, businessman, and well-known speaker—has traveled across the nation like a latter-day Pied Piper, sharing his compelling story—a legend that gave point to his life, history writ large and larger still in the telling. To every city, he carries with him a message of hope, hard work, good citizenship, and fighting for civil rights—all the attributes his hero had symbolized. Jackie Robinson gave Ronnie Rabinovitz the time of his life, as he gave his life to all time.

THE JACKIE ROBINSON RECORD

- Broke baseball's color barrier by making his major-league debut on April 15, 1947

- Named baseball's Rookie of the Year, 1947, an award that now bears his name

- Named *The Sporting News* Rookie of the Year, 1947

- National League's MVP, 1949, hitting .342 and driving in 124 runs

- Career batting average: .311

- Led the National League in steals twice; stole home 19 times in his career

- Elected to baseball's Hall of Fame (with Bob Feller) on the first ballot, 1962

- Awarded the Presidential Medal of Freedom, 1984

- Honorary election to the Canadian Baseball Hall of Fame, 1991

BIBLIOGRAPHY

Eig, Jonathan. *Opening Day: The Story of Jackie Robinson's First Season*. New York: Simon & Schuster, 2007.

Helgeland, Brian. *42: The True Story of an American Legend*. DVD. Directed by Brian Helgeland. Burbank, Calif.: Warner Bros., 2013.

Jackie Robinson & the Kid: A Story of Friendship, Courage, and Adversity. Press kit.

Rabinovitz Correspondence. Private collection.

Rampersad, Arnold. *Jackie Robinson: A Biography*. New York: Knopf, 1997.

Robinson, Jackie. *I Never Had It Made: An Autobiography*. With Alfred Duckett. Hopewell, N.J.: Ecco Press, 1995. First published 1972 by Putnam.

Robinson, Rachel. *Jackie Robinson: An Intimate Portrait*. With Lee Daniels. Rev. ed. New York: Abrams, 2014.

Robinson, Sharon. *Stealing Home: An Intimate Family Portrait by the Daughter of Jackie Robinson*. New York: HarperCollins, 1996.

To learn more about Ronnie and Jackie's relationship, visit www.ronrabinovitz.com.

Chock full o' Nuts
REG. U.S. PAT. OFF.

425 LEXINGTON AVENUE
New York 17, N. Y.

Dear Ronnie,

It was good hearing from you again. I hope every one is fine at home. My family is fine. We have had a nice summer and with school just around the corner we are getting prepared.

It looks as if the Dodgers have blown their chance. On paper they look like the best club but there doesn't seem to be the spark when its needed most. Its good to know you are still keeping close to the game and you have friends on the club, give them my regards.

You are very kind to say the nice things you did. I learned a long time ago that a person must be true to himself if he is to succeed. He must be willing to stand by his principles even at the possible loss of prestige. He must first learn to live with himself before he can hope to live with others. I have been fortunate, God has been good to me and I intend to work as hard as I can to repay all the things people have done for me.

I appreciate your friendship and feel as long as you set a worthwhile goal and head for it you will do well. Continued good luck. Give my regards to the family.

always
Jack